GREAT MYSTERIES

Angels

OPPOSING VIEWPOINTS®

Look for these and other exciting *Great Mysteries: Opposing Viewpoints* books:

GREAT MYSTERIES

Angels

OPPOSING VIEWPOINTS®

by Deanne Durrett

Greenhaven Press, Inc.   P.O. Box 289009, San Diego, California 92198-9009

Library of Congress Cataloging-in-Publication Data

Durrett, Deanne, 1940–
    Angels : opposing viewpoints / by Deanne Durrett.
        p. cm. — (Great mysteries)
    Includes bibliographical references and index.
    ISBN 1-56510-353-X   (alk. paper)
    1. Angels—Juvenile literature.   I. Title.   II. Series: Great
mysteries (Saint Paul, Minn.)
BL477.D87   1996
291.2'15—dc20   95-35981
                                          CIP
                                          AC

To My Mother
June Grantham

Acknowledgments

The author wishes to thank June Grantham, Barbara
Strong, and Shirley Garneau for sharing their experiences and Rasheed Gadir and Fouad Khadija for
their knowledge of Islamic beliefs.

Contents

Introduction

This book is written for the curious—those who want to explore the mysteries that are everywhere. To be human is to be constantly surrounded by wonderment. How do birds fly? Are ghosts real? Can animals and people communicate? Was King Arthur a real person or a myth? Why did Amelia Earhart disappear? Did history really happen the way we think it did? Where did the world come from? Where is it going?

Great Mysteries: Opposing Viewpoints books are intended to offer the reader an opportunity to explore some of the many mysteries that both trouble and intrigue us. For the span of each book, we want the reader to feel that he or she is a scientist investigating the extinction of the dinosaurs, an archaeologist searching for clues to the origin of the great Egyptian pyramids, a psychic detective testing the existence of ESP.

One thing all mysteries have in common is that there is no ready answer. Often there are *many* answers but none on which even the majority of authorities agrees. *Great Mysteries: Opposing Viewpoints* books introduce the intriguing views of the experts, allowing the reader to participate in their explorations, their theories, and their disagreements as they try to explain the mysteries of our world.

But most readers won't want to stop here. These *Great Mysteries: Opposing Viewpoints* aim to stimulate the reader's curiosity. Although truth is often impossible to discover, the search is fascinating. It is up to the reader to examine the evidence, to decide whether the answer is there—or to explore further.

"Penetrating so many secrets, we cease to believe in the unknowable. But there it sits nevertheless, calmly licking its chops."

H.L. Mencken, American essayist

Foreword

Angels at Mons

In 1914, shortly after the outbreak of World War I, the massive German army swept across Belgium, planning to surround France. In August of that same year, British soldiers joined the French effort to halt the German offensive. Day by day, as the relentless German forces surged ahead, the situation grew more bleak. Toward the end of August, as the Allies retreated, one small contingent of British soldiers found itself outnumbered by German forces and cut off from their French allies. With little hope of survival, the soldiers bravely fought to hold their position near Mons, Belgium. Mrs. St. John Mildmay reported this eyewitness account in the August 1915 issue of the *North American Review*: "300,000 Germans . . . with all their artillery swelled like a flood against the little English [British] Army, and not only was it a time of danger, not merely of defeat, but of utter annihilation."

Sudden Hope

The shelling intensified. The German attackers rode within three hundred feet of the British trenches. As the British soldiers prepared to die, some saw a sudden flash, then the oncoming horses bolted and turned. Wave after wave of gray-uniformed German riders fell. When at last the guns

(Opposite page) Angelic archers fend off advancing German troops in this 1915 portrayal of the Battle of Mons.

fell silent, the battle ended as the remaining German soldiers fled.

Later, after the French and British wounded had arrived at the field hospital, they gave extraordinary accounts of their miraculous rescue.

A lance corporal told his nurse that he had seen a strange light in the air. As the light became brighter, he could see three beings dressed in loose-fitting golden robes. The largest one had outstretched wings. These glowing beings seemed to hover above the German lines facing the British. Other men gave similar accounts, which were reported in the *Literary Digest* on September 25, 1915: "The moment it [the luminous cloud] appeared the German onslaught received a check. The horses could be seen rearing and plunging, and ceased to advance."

A year after the incident at Mons, Private Robert Cleaver, a British soldier of the First Cheshire Regiment, made a deposition under oath. He stated: "I personally was at Mons and saw the vision of angels with my own eyes." He described a "flash" that faded away after the advancing German cavalry had been halted.

Different Visions

British, French, and German soldiers gave accounts of the strange happening although interpretations of the vision differed. French soldiers reported seeing the archangel Michael riding a white horse, while the British identified the rider as St. George. German soldiers reported an encounter with thousands of Allied troops, while in reality there had been only hundreds. The September 20, 1915, issue of the *Independent* (a magazine published in the United States) quoted a German lieutenant as saying:

> I only know that we were charging full on the British at a certain place, and in a moment we were stopped. It was most like going full speed

and being pulled up suddenly on a precipice, but there was no precipice there, nothing at all, only our horses swerved around and fled and we could do nothing!

Credible Sources?

A few months later, the Reverend A. A. Boddy, vicar of All Saints' Church in Sunderland, England, visited the front and investigated the event by

A line of bowmen protect struggling British troops during the Battle of Mons. Soldiers described seeing different visions that day, with some seeing well-known angels and others encountering invisible forces.

questioning the troops. The reports he heard supported one another and came from reliable sources.

Or Hysteria Generated by Pulp Fiction?

About the time Great Britain entered the war, Arthur Machen, a writer for the London *Evening News*, wrote a series of short stories about the battlefront. One of his first stories, called "The Bowmen," seemed to parallel the accounts of the angel at Mons. In this story the British are overwhelmed by a German attack. At the bleakest moment, St. George suddenly appears with an army of "shining" bowmen to aid the desperate British troops in defending themselves against the massive German army. Although Machen claimed that he wrote "The Bowmen" purely from his imagination, the public believed the event to be true. Those who wanted to believe that angels appeared at Mons found support for their belief.

Skeptics readily linked the reports of the sighting of angels at Mons to Machen's fictitious "Bowmen." They labeled the sighting as hysteria resulting from the influence of the emotion-packed story. However, eyewitness accounts from the battlefield at Mons had begun to circulate in France a month before the London *Evening News* published Machen's story of the bowmen.

Who can decide? Was it rumor or truth; divine intervention or hallucination? What was seen in that glowing mist? Why did the German army flee as they neared victory?

To this day many people have no trouble at all believing angels appeared at Mons. With the world in a state of war, people needed encouragement. Is this not the role of angels: to inspire and encourage? Others, however, are a bit more skeptical. They explain away the tale as rumor resulting from overstimulated imaginations during a time of crisis. However, the eyewitness accounts are not so easily discredited. Hallucinations are seen by one person,

"A beautiful story . . . about the [sighting] of angels in defense of the British at Mons has arisen and found credence in England and even in the United States."

The Independent, September 20, 1915

"[The Mons story] presents a curious mixture of circumstantial statement that might conceivably be true and of literary fancy that is admittedly fiction."

Editorial in *The Christian Commonwealth*, London, ca. 1915

but many people saw the angels at Mons. The soldiers of three armies, in fact, saw the angels. While skeptics argue on the side of hallucination and rumors gone wild, believers remain sure of divine intervention.

Do angels exist? Eyewitness accounts from the beginning of time certainly suggest a strong belief that they do. Nevertheless, skeptics demand proof that no one has been able to provide.

One

Angels Throughout History

Almost all nations and cultures throughout history have believed in spirit beings. These beings freely traverse the distance and space between the unseen spirit world and the physical world, the realm in which we live. Evidence of this belief has been passed from generation to generation orally, carved on stone pillars of ancient temples and tombs, and written on clay tablets and parchment scrolls.

Some scholars contend that the earliest stone carving representing an angel was found in the ruins of Ur. The Bible identifies this ancient city, located on the Euphrates River in the area now known as Iraq, as the early home of Abraham, the first patriarch, or ancestor, of the Hebrew people. In the carving found in the ruins of the ancient city, a winged figure descends from the heavens to pour water into the cup of a king. Other ancient depictions of winged creatures that possibly represent angelic beings have been found in Mesopotamia, Egypt, Greece, and many areas of Asia Minor.

Angelologists (religious scholars who study angels) contend that these beings are not the same as the spiritual beings called angels by the three major Western religions: Judaism, Christianity, and Islam. Modern beliefs about angels, secular as well as

(Opposite page) Many cultures throughout history have believed that angels are celestial beings who travel between the spiritual and physical realms.

religious, are based on the ancient holy books of these religions.

The word *angel* comes from the Greek word *angelos* (translated from the Hebrew word *mal'ak*), which means "messenger." Angels are messengers and servants of the one God worshiped by followers of these three Western religions.

Judaism

The roots of Judaism, Christianity, and Islam reach back four thousand years to the time of Abraham. The oldest holy book of these religions, called the Old Testament, is the history of the Hebrew people. It contains the writings of many Hebrew leaders and prophets, which they believed were inspired by the revelations of God himself. In the Old Testament account of the establishment of the Jewish re-

Abraham encounters three angels. In both the Old and the New Testaments, angels were often messengers who relayed warnings and announcements.

The first biblical account of an angel appearing to a person was recorded in Genesis, the first book of the Old Testament. In this narrative, Hagar, the maidservant of Sarai, is visited by the angel of the Lord.

ligion, known as Judaism, angels appeared and reappeared. The multiple appearances firmly established Jewish belief in these messengers of God.

Old Testament angels usually took on the appearance of men, but in most cases the person seeing these beings recognized them as angels. Sometimes angels in the Old Testament appeared in supernatural circumstances. Once, for example, the angel of the Lord (God) appeared in the flames of a burning bush.

Genesis, the first book of the Old Testament (probably written by the early Hebrew leader Moses, in about 1440 B.C.), gives the first biblical account of an angel appearing to a person. The angel appeared to Hagar, the maidservant of Sarai. According to the Bible, Sarai (also known as Sarah) had been unable to have children. Wanting Abram (also known as Abraham) to have an heir, Sarai allowed him to take Hagar as a second wife. When Hagar became pregnant, Sarai, overwhelmed with jealousy, mistreated her. In order to escape Sarai's wrath, Hagar fled to the desert. There the angel of the Lord found her and told her to return home. The angel seemed to speak the direct words of God and not only assured Hagar of her safety upon returning home but also told her she would bear many children.

Many figures in the Old Testaments encountered angels. The voice of an angel stopped Abraham from sacrificing his son, Isaac. Angels also warned Lot to take his family and flee before God destroyed the evil cities of Sodom and Gomorrah with fire. Angels served as helpers and protectors to the descendants of Abraham.

Christianity

About two thousand years ago, some Jews began to follow a new leader, Jesus Christ. They believed that Jesus was the Son of God, and that his birth had been predicted in the Old Testament. These followers of Christ formed a new religion called Christianity. They began to record the teachings of Jesus and an account of the establishment of the church. Many years later, the writings of these early Christians became the New Testament. The Old Testament and New Testament make up the holy book of the Christian religion, the Bible.

The early Christians readily accepted the Old Testament accounts of angels into their new religion, and there are many references to angels in the New Testament. An angel told Mary that she would have a baby who would be the Son of God. A few months later another angel announced the birth of Jesus to shepherds in a field. The angels watched over Jesus throughout his life on earth. Although the angels were silent during Jesus' crucifixion (death on the cross), an angel stood by at the empty tomb to announce his resurrection (return to life after dying). According to New Testament accounts, forty days after Jesus came back to life, he ascended (rose) into heaven. After his followers had watched Jesus disappear into the sky, two men (angels) dressed in white suddenly appeared. These holy messengers said that Jesus would return the same way his followers had seen him go.

The followers of Jesus, called disciples or apostles, saw angels many times after his death and mention angels often in their writings. Many of these writings are included as books of the New Testament. In fact, writers of the Old and New Testaments mention angels about three hundred times.

Islam

Islam, the third religion based on the beliefs of Abraham, followed the teachings of the Old Testament but added its own holy book, the Koran. The Koran refers to angels more than ninety times. According to Islamic tradition, the angel Jibril (the same as the Hebrew angel known as Gabriel)

Sitting by the empty tomb, an angel informs Christian followers of Jesus' resurrection.

revealed the Koran to their prophet Muhammad, who lived from 570 to 632, about six centuries after the establishment of Christianity. Muslims, people who practice the Islamic religion, believe the Koran is the word of God and that it restores them to the original religion of Abraham. They do not view Islam as a new religion. Muslims, like Christians and Jews, accept the existence of angels, but their view of how angels interact with humans differs from the Jewish and Christian beliefs, as reflected by accounts in the Koran.

Muslims believe angels are active in their daily lives. Two angels accompany each person continually; one records the person's good deeds and the other records his or her bad deeds. Muslims believe angels aid them in battle and question each person in his or her grave. The angel of death is present when a person dies and escorts the soul into the spiritual realm.

Many Jews, Christians, and Muslims unquestionably accept the existence of angels. However, these celestial (heavenly) beings remain a mystery even to those who believe. What are they? How do they exist? What is their nature? Why are they so seldom seen? How do they suddenly appear and just as suddenly vanish? Are they, in fact, seen at all, or are they merely imagined?

"Those who disbelieve in the Hereafter name the angels with the names of females."

The Koran 53:27

The view into the spiritual realm is described by the words of the apostle Paul: "For now we see through a glass, darkly . . ." The view is not clear enough to answer the many questions that arise about angels. One way to see how people have thought about angels through the centuries is through the art of the times.

Medieval Times

"Angels are pure spirits and so should be presumed to be bodiless and, hence, sexless."

Gastav Davidson, *A Dictionary of Angels*

The ancient Jews did not believe in portraying angels in pictures. They feared becoming involved in idolatry, the worship of idols or statues. As a result, throughout the ages of the Old Testament, images of angels and their activities were expressed in words only.

However, as Christianity spread throughout Europe in the fourth and fifth centuries, Christians abandoned the taboo against depicting the holy angels. Architects began adorning white stone churches with two-dimensional angels above the doors and on the pillars.

By the eighth century the Council of Nicaea (a meeting at the ancient city of Nicaea in the area now known as Turkey that established policy for the whole Christian Church) formally approved the use of angel images in the church. These images were considered worthy of respect and reverence but were not worshiped. Church leaders believed that the artistic images of angels would remind worshipers that the heavenly hosts (angels) participate in the sacraments (rites such as baptism and communion) of the church. Medieval artists continued to follow the tradition of the Old Testament, and depicted masculine angels wielding swords to represent their power and strength.

Renaissance

By the Renaissance (a revival of art and literature during the fourteenth, fifteenth, and sixteenth centuries in Europe) artists began to draw the three-dimensional figure, and the depiction of angels reached its full glory. The church and state began to compete to build grander churches and more elaborate palaces adorned with angels soaring and floating over ceilings, walls, and altar pieces. Angels became a favorite artistic form for displaying an artist's ability to create depth and perspective.

The Renaissance was also a time of renewed interest in the mythology of the ancient Greeks and Romans. Painters began to mix images of the pagan gods and goddesses of mythology with Christian angels, and angels became more feminine, more realistic, and more earthy. Plump cherub babies with tiny

By the seventeenth century, many religious denominations taught that the purpose of angels was to escort souls to heaven. Even today, it is commonplace for angels and cherubs to appear on headstones.

wings replaced the fierce cherubim (angels) with flaming swords described in Genesis. Since pictures are often more powerful than words, and since paintings and sculptures of angels were more accessible to people who often could not read, the artists' view became the way people thought of angels.

Protestant Rebellion

In the sixteenth century, many people became dissatisfied with the Catholic Church, which was the only Western Christian church up to that time. These people broke away and began forming their own small groups. People in these groups were called Protestants because they protested against the Catholic Church. Many of the denominations we know today, such as Lutheran, Calvinist, and Anglican, were formed at this time. Many Protestants objected to the elaborate and ornate Catholic churches. Therefore, they abolished angel figures from their new churches. They also placed less emphasis on the angelic role in human life. By the seventeenth century, in the Protestant view the main role of an angel was to escort the soul to heaven. Banished from the sanctuary (the large room in the church where services are held), winged angelic figures were now chiseled on tombstones, where they hovered over the dead.

Victorian Era

By the nineteenth century the popular view of angels had changed again. However, to understand this new view of angels, it is necessary to discuss the social and economic climate of the time. The industrial revolution represented the promise for a new life. Many people moved from rural areas to the cities in search of jobs in the new factories. These jobs, however, paid low wages and the cost of city living was higher than it was in rural communities. Many people actually became poorer when they moved to the city and took factory jobs. Their poverty became highly visible as slums developed in the inner cities.

Perhaps in an effort to deny the reality of hungry and sick children, artists began to paint healthy, rosy-cheeked cherubs and beautiful, fair-skinned, feminine angels. The beautiful Victorian angel nestled among ribbons, lace, and flowers became popular. These angels represented hope and encouragement. In addition, advancements in printing techniques made art prints more affordable, and many homes were decorated with pictures of beautiful angels.

Twentieth Century

Early in the twentieth century, war broke out in Europe and soon engulfed the nations of the world. The French and British fought bravely against the

"[Accounts such as those of the angels at Mons] testify to the natural mysticism of the natural man, who must bring God into his affairs, and who derives a peculiar spiritual satisfaction from stories which still await satisfactory demonstration of their objective truth."

Editorial in *The Christian Commonwealth*, London

"I am well aware that many will say that no one can possibly speak with spirits and angels so long as he is living in the body: many say it is all fancy, others that I recount such things to win credence, while others will make other kinds of objection. But I am deterred by none of these: for I have seen, I have heard, I have felt."

Emanuel Swedenborg, eighteenth-century philosopher and scientist advancing German army. Accounts of the angel at Mons swept through Europe, and each account seemed to prove that believers see angels as they believe them to be. The French saw the angel at Mons as the archangel Michael, and the British saw St. George, who was the patron saint of England.

While English clergymen in Manchester, Weymouth, and Herford claimed to have friends who confirmed the sighting at Mons, not everyone viewed the Mons visions as miraculous. A London minister, Dean Hensen, preached a sermon in Westminster Abbey in which he referred to the reports of the angel at Mons as "groveling superstition." Writers in the *Christian Commonwealth* (a London newspaper) wrote at the time:

> Many constitutional skeptics and many serious students and religious teachers . . . fear a return of superstition . . . [and] that democratic liberty

To offset the social and economic despair of the nineteenth century, Victorian artists painted playful cherubs and beautiful angels to offer hope and encouragement.

in Europe would be dearly purchased at the price of a revival of belief in angels, supernatural interventions, and miracles.

Without the complete support of religious leaders, the story of Mons faded away, as did interest in angels, until the latter part of the twentieth century.

In the early 1970s, while preparing a sermon on angels, the Reverend Billy Graham discovered he had no books in his library on the subject. As he checked further, he found that little had been written about angels in the twentieth century. Viewing this as a "strange and ominous omission," in 1975 Billy Graham wrote a book entitled *Angels: God's Secret Agents*. By the time the second edition was published in 1986, over two million copies had been sold.

Toward the end of the twentieth century, accounts of angel appearances began to circulate. Angel books enjoyed such popularity that bookstores devoted complete sections to the subject.

The late-twentieth-century angel—kind, loving, and friendly—became a new angel and a major player in the New Age movement (a growing interest in reaching spirit beings, through mysticism, channeling, crystals, and other substances). Talking about angels and sharing accounts of personal experiences and angel sightings became popular pastime. Slowly, as the New Age movement seemed to open a window to the spirit world, Christians, too, began to peek through. New Christian books on angels joined Billy Graham's book on shelves already crowded with New Age angel books. Angel merchandise also found its way to customers from all walks of life.

In 1975 the Reverend Billy Graham wrote a book entitled *Angels: God's Secret Agents*. This book renewed interest in the divine beings, selling over two million copies in eleven years.

Two

Angels Today

Angels are the fad of the 1990s. The first lady, Hillary Clinton, wears a small gold angel pin on her collar on days when she expects to cope with difficult problems. Marcia Clark, the prosecutor in the heavily publicized 1995 murder trial of O. J. Simpson, appeared in court wearing an angel on her lapel. From the White House to the courts to children's nurseries, images of angels abound.

Television Craze

Everyone wants to know about or tell about angels. As a result, radio and television talk show hosts actively seek guests who have seen angels, claim to have talked to them, or help others contact them. By October 1994 Oprah Winfrey had presented the subject of angels three times and talk show hosts Phil Donahue and Rolanda Watts had featured the subject of angels on their shows as well. One television series, *Touched by an Angel*, features stories of a fictional angel, and documentary programming reenacts experiences of those who claim to have encountered angels. In 1994, ABC aired "Angels: The Mysterious Messengers," a two-hour prime-time special hosted by actress Patty Duke. This documentary examined the subject of angels and reported angel experiences.

(Opposite page) Today, television shows, magazines, and even high-profile individuals have been caught up in the angel craze. Here, Hillary Clinton wears a gold angel pin while campaigning for her husband.

In addition, angel stories grace the pages of some of America's most influential magazines, including *Time*, *Newsweek*, *Ladies' Home Journal*, *Reader's Digest*, and *Redbook*. The subject has captured scarce newspaper space in some of the largest dailies. In response to the growing popularity of angels, Eileen Elias Freeman established the Angel-Watch Foundation in 1992 and began publishing a newsletter devoted to reporting angel activities around the world. Freeman mailed the first issue to fifty-five subscribers. By October 1994 her mailing list had grown to more than four thousand, with subscribers in the United States, Canada, Mexico, Argentina, Brazil, the Philippines, Guam, and nine countries in Europe.

Boutiques

In recent years retailers have opened angel boutiques that sell nothing but angel merchandise—everything from angel figurines and jewelry to baby rattles adorned with angel images. According to the *Los Angeles Times*, Sally Allen's Angels for All Seasons, a store in Denver, Colorado, that opened in September 1993, did $150,000 in business in its first four months of operation. By late 1994 more than 120 angel boutiques had opened across America, many of them doing an enormous business.

Many of the angel boutiques, including Tara's Angels in San Juan Capistrano, California, and the Blue Angel Boutique in British Columbia, opened as a result of personal experiences of the owners.

A blue angel visited Shirley Garneau's daughter, Nadina, daily when she was a small child, but disappeared when the child was about seven. Years later the angel returned, promising to become visible to her any time Nadina needed counsel or help. By that time Nadina had become an artist and the angel inspired her work as well as the opening of the Blue Angel Boutique.

As news of angel experiences spread, many people wanted to learn more about angels. Harvard Divinity School offered a course on angels, and Boston College boasted two. People who were not college students also wanted to learn about angels. To meet this need, New Age followers presented angel seminars in cities and rural retreats throughout America. Some of these workshops encouraged the attendees to share their experiences; others promised to teach people how to communicate with angels.

Angel Workshops

The methods varied from one workshop to another and often included influences from Eastern religions and ancient cultures. Some workshops emphasized the use of meditation and visualization; others taught participants to use an "angel oracle" to make contact with celestial beings. In meditation, students practice clearing their minds to receive thoughts from angels. In visualization, they use their imaginations to see with the mind's eye. According to the New Age view, this invisible eye, sometimes called the third eye, is located in the center of the forehead and is a person's link to the spiritual world.

The angel oracle consists of three lists. The first list contains names of the archangels (higher in rank than ordinary angels). The second contains sixteen different kinds of angels, such as companion angels and information angels. The third list contains places or circumstances where the angel might make contact. In order to use the oracle or "do a reading," readers close their eyes and allow their left index fingers to point to a selection from each list. The oracle may be used several times before contact is made. Eventually, it is thought, the chosen archangel (first list) will dispatch the kind of angel chosen (second list) to connect with the person in the chosen situation (third list).

"So you need someone you can trust, maybe your own guardian angel, someone you can call down yourself."

Marv Meyer, religious studies professor at Chapman University

"It's not up to us to see angels. It's up to the angels to reveal themselves to us."

Sophy Burnham in *Angels: The Mysterious Messengers*

Some critics point out that the techniques taught in an angel workshop are similar to those used to contact the dead through a séance and seem more related to superstition and the occult than to the heavenly hosts. This makes many in the Christian community wary. Gary Kinnaman, senior pastor of Word of Grace Church in Mesa, Arizona, expresses this view in his book, *Angels Dark and Light*: "To many people, like the authors of New Age angel books, an angel is an angel is an angel. No distinction is made between good and evil angels." A desire to avoid the possibility of being deceived by fallen angels masquerading as angels of light has slowed the Christian interest in climbing on the angel bandwagon. In fact, many aspects of the fascination with angels are completely contrary to religious beliefs of the Abrahamic religions.

The New Age

New Age views of angels fit quite well into nontraditional religious thinking, however. Followers of the New Age movement believe the world is on the threshold of a great expansion of consciousness and human development. Many of them believe angels are the link to the spiritual world. People who have attained the needed level of spirituality claim to be able to channel angels. Channeling means an individual goes into a trance, and the angel communicates—speaks or writes—through him or her. As a result, the angel can communicate with many people by making contact with only one person.

On a more personal level, many New Age followers like the idea of developing a relationship with their own individual guardian angels. Such a relationship seems to fill the need for a relationship with God. People find it easy to relate to angels. They see these spirits as loving and kind, devoted to nurturing personal growth and welfare. The authors of *Ask Your Angels*, Alma Daniel, Timothy Wyllie, and Andrew Ramer, believe angels "are here to help us raise our

Many people believe that angels are kind, loving spirits who are devoted to nurturing personal growth and well-being. Currently, both New Age followers and some religious people are apt to seek guidance from a guardian angel.

loving understanding and they connect with us at the highest level at which we are capable of functioning."

As this understanding is expanded some people believe they can become angels themselves. These people seek contact with guides to accompany them on their spiritual journeys. As they travel through one level of spirituality to the next, they believe they may become pure spirits, or angels. They give themselves angelic names and identify themselves as angels of light.

Why Do People Want to Believe in Guardian Angels?

The interest generated by the New Age enthusiasts seems to have made religious people more comfortable in talking about their own angel beliefs and experiences. Stories long kept secret have begun to surface. Suddenly it is acceptable to wonder if a kind stranger might have been an angel in human form, or if invisible hands reached out to prevent an accident. Why has talking about angels become acceptable in many social circles?

Some say the willingness to believe in angels is a function of the times. Television bombards people with frightening news right in their living rooms. As a result, millions of viewers become eyewitnesses to neighborhood violence, terrorist bombings, devastating earthquakes, and floods. People are more aware than ever before of lurking dangers. In a time where daily life can be very frightening, the thought of a powerful, invisible guardian standing nearby appeals to the nonreligious as well as the religious. Everyone wants comfort and assurance. As a result, more people are believing in the unseen, and some are seeing what they believe.

To many, angels seem easier to reach than God. People can have their own personal guardian angels devoted to their individual needs. In addition, angels do not make demands. They offer spirituality but do not require obedience or worship in return. As *Time* magazine suggests, "For those who choke too easily on God and his rules . . . angels are the handy compromise, all fluff and meringue, kind, nonjudgmental. And they are available to everyone."

The Position of the Church

Until well into the 1990s, Christian writers of both fiction and nonfiction paid far more attention to the work of Satan and spiritual warfare than to personal encounters with members of the heavenly host. Protestant ministers spoke of biblical angels from the pulpit, but seldom, if ever, was the topic of personal guardian angels the subject of a sermon. Eventually, however, the overwhelming interest in the subject of angels attracted the attention of the

"Angels are reassurance that the supernatural and the realm of God are real."

Richard Woods, Dominican priest and author of books on angels and demons

"Angels too easily provide a temptation for those who want a 'fix' of spirituality without bothering with God Himself."

Timothy Jones and Andrew J. Bandstra, *Christianity Today*

In response to overwhelming interest in angels, Dr. David Jeremiah, pastor of the Shadow Mountain Community Church, began a series of sermons on angels in May 1995.

pulpit. In May 1995, Dr. David Jeremiah, pastor of the Shadow Mountain Community Church, a large Baptist church in El Cajon, California, and minister of Turning Point Radio and Television Ministry, began a series of sermons on angels.

The mainstream religious community has refused to be caught up in angelmania, and the position of angels in church doctrine remains the same. Those who hold to fundamental religious beliefs compare personal accounts of angel encounters to the angel encounters recorded in the Scriptures. If the angel carries a message contrary to biblical teachings, the source of the angel is suspect. Many Christians exercise caution, balancing themselves between the warnings of St. Paul ("For Satan himself masquerades as an angel of light") and the promise of David ("The angel of the Lord encamps around those who fear him, and delivers them").

Three

What Are Angels?

Tara, the teenage daughter of Kirk and Sandy Moore of San Juan Capistrano, California, loved angels. The teenager died in a tragic automobile accident in August 1992. The day after the accident, the Moores found an angel cookie Tara had made and sheet music bearing the title *I Am an Angel* on the floor in her room. Convinced that these items were messages from Tara, the Moores, as a tribute to their daughter, opened a store that sells only angel merchandise. "We wanted to change our lives after the tragedy and make a statement that would carry on Tara's memory," said Mr. Moore. "I know she has seen the store. I can feel her energy in there."

Is Tara now among the angels? The belief that humans become angels is not acceptable to everyone. However, where angels are concerned many different views exist.

Theologians (religious scholars) and lay people (nonpreachers) have speculated about the nature of angels for hundreds of generations but have arrived at few definite answers. Many people agree that the most reliable source of information about angels is the Bible.

According to the apostle Paul's writings in the New Testament, God created angels, ". . . whether they be thrones, or dominions, or principalities or

(Opposite page) Throughout history, theologians and lay people have theorized about the nature of angels. Although there are many differing views, the Bible states that angels are messengers from God who help and protect people.

powers: all things were created by him [God], and for him." Christians believe the thrones, dominions, principalities, and powers are ranks of angels. Other ranks or types of angels mentioned in the Bible are seraphim, cherubim, mights (sometimes called virtues), authorities, archangels, and angels. Among these ranks are the fearless and powerful spiritual creatures described in the Old Testament, which do not resemble the kind and beautiful beings we have come to recognize as angels today.

According to the Bible, God created the angels a little higher than humans to serve as messengers from God and to help and protect people.

Islamic beliefs are similar. Muslims believe God created angels from light before the creation of humans.

Not Human

Most Bible scholars agree that angels are not human or even like humans. The Bible teaches that angels do not possess physical bodies, although they are reported to sometimes take on human form in order to perform a task assigned by God. They have the ability to change their appearance and to go from one place to another in an instant. They appear and disappear, or step from the invisible world into the visible world at will.

According to the Bible and the Koran, angels are neither male nor female and do not marry or reproduce. However, the Book of Enoch, another account from biblical times, gives details of a super race of giants that resulted from the union of the sons of God, thought to be angels, and the daughters of humans. The Bible also makes reference to this race of giants. Some controversy exists concerning the meaning of "sons of God." Some think the term refers to rulers and judges, since these people were sometimes called gods in the Hebrew language. Others theorize that there may be an additional rank of angel, called watchers, that possesses gender traits.

"For by him [God] were all things created, that are in heaven, and that are in earth, visible and invisible, whether they be thrones, or dominions, or principalities or powers: all things were created by him, and for him."

The Bible, Colossians 1:16 (King James Version)

"[Remember] that we create what we believe. Indeed, I am prepared to say that if enough of us believe in angels, then angels exist."

Gastav Davidson, *A Dictionary of Angels*

Although many people agree that God created angels as a separate creature, completely unrelated to humans, others contend that the human soul becomes an angel upon death. This was the belief of Joseph Smith, who encountered an angel at Palmyra, New York, in 1823. This angel identified himself as Moroni. He claimed to be a descendant of a group of ancient Hebrews who immigrated to America long before the establishment of the Christian religion. In the fifth century, Moroni, as the last of his race, hid the records of his people for safekeeping. Upon his death he became an angel. In his nineteenth-century appearance to Joseph Smith, the angel Moroni revealed the hiding place of the records imprinted on the gold plates he had buried shortly before his death. With the use of the *urim* and *thummim* (mysterious objects mentioned in the Old Testament that are used for understanding God's will) that were found with the gold tablets, Smith translated the text of the Book of Mormon and founded the Church of Jesus Christ of Latter-Day Saints.

In 1823, Joseph Smith (pictured) reported that he was visited by Moroni, an angel who claimed to have lived during the fifth century. Following the encounter, Smith translated the Book of Mormon and founded the Church of Jesus Christ of Latter-Day Saints.

Not Beings but Ideas

Although most believers agree that angels are spiritual beings, some people think of angels as ideas or thoughts. In other words, an angel is the message itself, not the messenger. Mary Baker Eddy, Christian Science founder, compared the concept of angels as humanlike beings with feathered wings to the image of freedom depicted in the Statue of Liberty. Eddy said, "Angels are not etherealized [intangible] human beings. . . . Angels are pure thoughts from God, winged with Truth and Love." To Mary Baker Eddy, angels existed only for a moment as a thought transferred from God to a person. In her view, angels are continually being created but do not continue to exist. Others, however, believe that all of the angels were created at one time and that none are added and none die. Still others believe the number of angels continually grows as humans die and become angels.

How Many Angels Are There?

Many people want to know how many angels exist. In the Islamic view the number of angels is so great that only God knows how many there are. The Bible offers some clues but does not answer the question. It numbers the angels in terms of tens of thousands, and ten thousand multiplied by ten thousand, which equals 100 million. In fact, there may be more than 100 million angels. In the Old Testament, Moses writes of "myriads of holy ones [angels]." Myriad means an infinite number, more than anyone can calculate. However, some people have tried.

In the thirteenth century, St. Albert the Great (Albertus Magnus), a German theologian and scientist, calculated that there were exactly 399,920,004 angels. In the next century, Kabbalists, followers of mystic teachings based on the Hebrew Scriptures, calculated the number of angels to be 301,655,722.

Clement of Alexandria, a Greek theologian born about A.D. 150, followed another line of thinking based on references in the Scripture associating angels with stars. His suggestion, that the number of angels equals the number of stars in the sky, implies there may be billions.

Orders of Angels

The Bible names nine different orders, or types, of angelic beings. It indicates that each is distinctive. Many scholars have studied the ancient writings and several have speculated on how angels rank. The works of Dionysius the Pseudo-Areopagite (judge) received high acclaim. Until about 1450 these works were thought to be based on firsthand knowledge of the teachings of the apostle Paul. At that time, scholars determined that an unknown Syrian who lived in the sixth century actually wrote them using

The title page from the book *The Hierarchie of the Blessed Angells,* which attempts to classify the nine orders of angels outlined in the Bible.

the name mentioned in the Bible. Once determined to be a fraud, the person writing under the name of Dionysius the Areopagite became known as Pseudo-Dionysius. According to Sophy Burnham, author of several best-selling books on angels:

> His [Dionysius] influence in the Middle Ages was enormous, and the best-known hierarchy [order] of angels is his. . . . Pseudo-Dionysius arranged the angels into three groupings, using [apostle] Paul's list, and everyone else took them up.

According to Dionysius, the angelic court ranks as follows:

(nearest to God)

Highest Triad

1. Seraphim   2. Cherubim   3. Thrones

Middle Triad

1. Dominions   2. Virtues   3. Powers

Lowest Triad

1. Principalities   2. Archangels   3. Angels

(nearest to humans)

What Do Angels Look Like?

Most reports of angel sightings suggest that angels usually take on an appearance of something familiar, another human, for example, or even an army, like the German soldiers saw at Mons. But what do angels look like in their natural form? General William Booth, founder of the Salvation Army, had a significant angelic vision. He described the angels in his vision as having an aura of rainbow light so bright that at full strength humans could not tolerate it.

In their natural form, angels have been described as having an aura of brilliant light. Jews believe that this radiance is the light of God.

Accounts in the New Testament agree with this description. In Matthew 28:3, the angel that rolled the stone from Jesus' tomb wore white and shone with dazzling brilliance like a flash of lightning.

In Judaism, angels are thought to be spiritual bodies filled with the light of God. "The light is like the spirit, and there's also something that contains the spirit—so there's a structure of the angel, but it's not a physical body," said Rabbi Yosef Levin of Chabad in Palo Alto, California. However, others think of angels in different terms.

Joseph Smith knew he was seeing a human soul who had become an angel when he met Moroni. The angel, surrounded by an aura of light, gave Smith the golden tablets containing the text of the *Book of Mormon.* Wingless and manly, a golden statue of the angel Moroni stands atop the spire of the Mormon temple in Salt Lake City today.

Muhammad agreed about the brilliance surrounding angels. He described them as beings created from pure, bright gems, brilliant and beautiful compared to the dull clay used to mold humans. Gabriel wore white robes when he visited Muhammad to deliver the Koran over the course of twenty-three years. However, when Muhammad asked God to send Gabriel in his natural form, the wings of the angel filled the sky.

Azreal is a death angel described in Muslim tradition as having seventy thousand feet and four thousand wings. Many eyes and tongues cover his body. The human mind cannot accurately imagine such a creature. In fact, the characteristics described as tongues, eyes, feet, and wings may not be these body parts at all, but some unknown features best described to humans in these terms.

Where Does This Information Come From?

Although angels are mentioned throughout the Bible, most of the information concerns what angels do, not what they are. For this reason, those who

This engraving from John Milton's *Paradise Lost* shows the angels Ithuriel and Zephon. Although written in the seventeenth century, Milton's masterpiece remains influential to modern writings about angels.

have tried to unravel the mystery have relied on other sources. One of these sources, the Book of Enoch, was written in Old Testament times, but is not part of the Holy Bible. Other sources of information about angels include ancient myths, legends, and folklore.

Many authors have mingled these sources together in an effort to determine what angels are. For example, Dante Alighieri's great epic poem *Divine Comedy*, written in the fourteenth century, and John Milton's poem *Paradise Lost*, written in the seventeenth century, are often quoted in modern writings about angels.

Into the Spiritual Realm

Other information about angels comes from the experiences of people who claim to know about them through extrasensory perception, that is, the ability to know or see things not usually apparent to humans. Emanuel Swedenborg, born in 1688, was a professor of theology at Uppsala, Sweden, and the bishop of Skara. He claimed to be able to see into the spiritual realm. Also a brilliant scientist, Swedenborg was appointed to the Swedish Board of Mines in 1714. In 1747 he resigned from the Board of Mines determined to devote himself to the study of angels. He learned Hebrew in order to study ancient texts, and he wrote freely of his communication with angels as he explored the spiritual realm.

The angels told him that they can express only love and cannot speak of doubt, conflict, and argument as humans do. Their power comes from God, and if they doubt the source of their power they become weak. Swedenborg thought that the bodies of angels were made of substances that do not reflect light in a way that is visible to humans. Changes had to take place before an angel could be seen by human eyes. Either the angel had to enter the physical world by taking on a physical body, or the spiritual eye of the beholder had to open and allow the person to see into the invisible world.

Rudolf Steiner, born in 1861 in Czechoslovakia, was a brilliant man of many talents. At the age of eight he realized that he saw worlds and creatures that ordinary people did not see. He kept his gift of "second sight" secret while educating himself in many fields, including natural history, mathematics, philosophy, the arts, architecture, medicine, education, and agriculture. Steiner was a philosopher as well as scientist, and spent much of his life thinking and writing about angels. He believed in reincarnation and claimed that every person has an angel that guides him or her through one lifetime after another. According to his beliefs, the influence of this personal angel is strongest in childhood. This influence fades in the early adult years and returns after middle age when the person again becomes more spiritual. Steiner also believed that an angel could reveal the person's past lifetimes when requested.

Many of the beliefs of Swedenborg and Steiner are reflected in contemporary writings by followers of the New Age movement.

The Swedish theologian and scientist Emanuel Swedenborg claimed he could see into the spiritual realm and communicate with angels.

Michael, the messenger of law and judgment, is considered to be the archangel in both the Jewish and Christian traditions.

The legends as well as the religious literature of many cultures describe angels and often name individual angels. Identifying angels by name, however, can be extremely confusing. The same angel seems to appear in the literature and lore of all three major religions, but under different names, credited with varying acts, and apparently belonging to several angelic orders. The named angels also appear as characters in classic literature, such as Milton's *Paradise Lost* and Dante's *Divine Comedy*.

The Protestant Bible names three angels— Michael, Gabriel, and Lucifer. The Catholic Bible adds Raphael to the list. The Hebrew Bible (Old Testament) names only Gabriel and Michael. The Islamic Koran names several angels, including Gabriel, Malik, Harut, Marut, and Iblis (counterpart of the Judeo-Christian Satan). Iblis seems to be counted among the angels when he refused to bow to Adam. However, he does not meet the Islamic criteria for angels: he is made from fire, not light, and he disobeyed God. According to Islamic beliefs, angels do not have a free will but must always obey God. Iblis, therefore, is considered to be a jinni (a spirit), not an angel.

With the dawning of the New Age, countless names have been added to the list of angels. Those who follow New Age beliefs seek encounters with angelic beings and often claim success in meeting their angels, offering the angel's name as proof. Some offer entirely new and strange names while others claim to have met the well-known archangel, Michael.

Michael

Michael is the highest ranking of all the angels who interact with humans in Jewish and Christian writings and most secular literature. According to Islamic beliefs, Michael is outranked by Gabriel, the angel who delivered the Koran to Muhammad.

The name *Michael* means "who is like unto the Lord," or "who is as God." The prefix *arch-* suggests high authority, the angel above all angels. Michael is considered the guardian angel of the nation of Israel. He is God's messenger of law and judgment. As such, he appears in Revelation, the last book of the Christian Bible, as he leads the armies of God against Satan: "And there was war in heaven. Michael and his angels fought against the dragon, and the dragon and his angels fought back."

According to the Talmud, Sarah recognized Michael as one of the three angels Abraham entertained under the oak tree. These angels brought the message that Sarah and Abraham would have a son although they were very old. The son was Isaac. Michael is also thought to be the angel who stopped Abraham from sacrificing Isaac. This story is recorded in the Old Testament's Book of Genesis.

Some Jewish scholars credit Michael as being the angel of the Lord that appeared in the flames of the bush that didn't burn. He told Moses to lead the Hebrew people out of Egypt where they were being held in slavery.

Islamic literature describes Michael as having wings of emerald green covered with saffron hairs, each wing with a million faces that cry out to God for pardon in a million dialects. As Michael cries for the sins of the faithful, cherubim form from his tears.

Joan of Arc claimed that Michael brought her the message that she should liberate France from England. As a result, she led the French armies in the Hundred Years' War and regained the throne of King Charles VII from the English.

Gabriel

The Hebrew name *Gabriel* means "God is my strength." One of the most prominent angels in the Bible, Gabriel serves primarily as God's messenger

According to the New Testament, Gabriel, the messenger of mercy and promise, informed Mary that she would give birth to the Son of God.

of mercy and promise. In the Book of Daniel in the Old Testament, he helps Daniel understand his prophetic vision. When Gabriel appears to Daniel again, Daniel recognizes him and reports that Gabriel flew swiftly, came close, and touched him.

In the New Testament, Gabriel announces the coming birth of John the Baptist to his unsuspecting parents. Then a few verses later, Gabriel informs the Virgin Mary that she will bear the Son of God.

The Old Testament describes Gabriel as carrying a sword as the angel of judgment. In other literature he is said to have destroyed the evil cities of

Sodom and Gomorrah. He also protected the infant Moses, the future leader of the Hebrew people, as the Egyptian princess pulled him, in his basket, from the Nile River.

Satan

Satan is the Hebrew word for "adversary," or opponent, competitor, or enemy. Some Christians believe Satan was once Lucifer, the brightest and best of all God's angels. However, when Lucifer saw that he was so much better than the other angels, he began to think he could raise himself above God. In the resulting battle Lucifer and one-third of the angels were thrown from heaven. Christians believe Satan continues in his battle with God by competing for the human soul. He uses deception (making wrong seem right) as he tempts humanity to disobey God. His most successful weapons are money, power, and lust.

Raphael

The Hebrew word *Raphael* means "God has healed." Raphael is found in the Book of Tobit. Although neither Jews nor Protestants accept this book as part of the Scriptures, Catholics include it in their canon. Catholics believe Raphael serves as supervisor of all guardian angels and that he specializes in healing and creativity.

Iblis

Iblis comes from the Greek word *diabolos*, which means "devil." Iblis is a Muslim counterpart of the Christian Satan. According to the Koran, when God created Adam, he ordered the angels to bow down to the first man. All the angels bowed except Iblis. Iblis, made of fire, argued that he was better than the man, who was made of lowly clay, and refused to bow. As punishment for his rebellion, Allah (God) banned Iblis from paradise. Seeking revenge, Iblis deceived the first woman, Hawwa, into eating the forbidden fruit. When Allah discovered what she had done, he cursed her with the pain of childbirth and cast her from paradise along with Adam. Although Iblis is counted among the angels, Muslims view him as a jinni or spirit that can take human form and influence human events.

Malik

Found in the Koran, *Malik* means "one who is in charge." According to Muslim beliefs, the angel Malik oversees hell. In the Koran, sinners imprisoned in hell cry out to Malik for death as a release from their suffering. However, Malik tells them they must remain in hell forever because they rejected

The Koran records that God ordered his angels to bow before Adam, the first man (pictured). Only one angel, Iblis, refused to bow and was cast out of paradise for his disobedience.

the truth. Under Malik's command, nineteen angels guard the boundaries of hell.

Harut and Marut

Islamic scholars disagree on the interpretation of the Koran regarding Harut and Marut. For example, Abdullah Yusuf Ali believes they were mortal men who are called angels because of their knowledge, wisdom, and power. S. Abdul A'la Maududi believes they were angels sent by God to tempt mankind.

Harut and Marut are credited with teaching either science or magic. Many people who came into possession of this knowledge used it for evil. For this reason Harut and Marut seemed to be teaching evil and appeared to behave like fallen angels. Muslims do not believe angels fall and therefore maintain that these angels remained virtuous and did not fall out of favor with God. According to Islamic tradition, they may have been men who possessed great knowledge and power or angels sent by God as tempters, but they were not fallen angels.

Tales of these angels named in the sacred books of the Muslim, Christian, and Jew also grace the pages of secular legend and lore. Some people believe the lore and some believe the sacred writings. Others see a mystery and search for the truth.

"Angels do not have wings."

Eileen Elias Freeman in *Angels: The Mysterious Messengers*

"They can appear with wing-like energy fields that we discern as wings."

K. Martin-Kuri, angelologist and artist

Four

Has Anyone Actually Seen an Angel?

Many people claim to have seen angels. These sightings can't be proved; they are believed on faith. Neither can skeptics disprove them, however, and few try.

One Old Testament account, found in the second Book of Kings, tells about the servant of the prophet Elisha, who awoke one morning to discover an enemy army surrounding them. The frightened servant cried to Elisha, "What shall we do?" Elisha assured him that God protected them with a force much stronger than that of the enemy. Elisha then prayed that God would allow the servant to see the army on their side. The servant's eyes, which had been blind to the spiritual world, opened to see the heavenly force protecting Elisha. The servant saw horses and chariots of fire filling the hills around them. Most biblical scholars agree that these were angels.

Many other examples of unseen angels watching over people are found in the Bible, as are several accounts of a few people who were allowed a brief look into the spiritual realm. Ron Rhodes of the Christian Research Institute in Irvine, California, wrote that like Elisha's servant,

> You and I may often be unaware of the presence of angels in our midst. There is no telling just

(Opposite page) Although many people claim to have encountered angels, these incidents cannot be proven. Nonetheless, faithful believers continue to assert that angels have touched their lives and given them a glimpse into the spiritual realm.

how many times God has kept us safe through the work of angels without us having known anything about it.

Many people today claim to have seen an angel. Books and magazine articles contain numerous accounts of their experiences. Other people, however, know within themselves they have encountered an angel and keep silent. Some feel the experience is too special to share, while others fear ridicule. Still other people experience unexplainable encounters and wonder if it could have been an angel that came to their aid.

Angel of Light

Denise Brumbach, who operates a beauty shop out of her home in Manheim, Pennsylvania, shared her experience with *Guidepost* magazine readers. Denise and her family befriended an inner-city youngster who wanted more than anything to go to school where he would be safe. The Brumbachs decided to help. However, after they managed to get Angel (his name) enrolled in school, business decreased at the beauty shop. The Brumbachs soon noticed that their customers and friends did not approve of Angel and were shunning them. The Brumbachs began to wonder if it was really worth the struggle to help Angel attend school.

One night, torn between protecting her family and business and wanting to help Angel, Denise prayed for an answer. Should they give up and ask Angel to leave? As she prayed, Denise noticed a glow at the far side of the kitchen. The glow quickly grew into blinding brilliance. Denise then received a clear and silent message, "Let him stay. It will be all right." The kitchen darkened as the light disappeared. Denise has no doubt that she had seen an angel.

Flowing Effervescence

In August 1993, the *San Francisco Examiner* reported Caroline Sutherland's angel experience. First

Denise Brumbach (left) believes she was visited by a divine being who told her to continue to help Angel (center), a disadvantaged inner-city youth.

to arrive for work, Caroline soon realized she was not alone. The room suddenly filled with heat and light. She looked up as the whole back wall fell away and a "12-foot-plus guardian-angel-being" appeared. The figure had wings and "a flowing effervescence aswirl in beautiful colors, like the aurora borealis. . . . The presence was so strong and so vibrant, and the room was filled with light and love. My heart was tingling," she said. In this thirty-second glimpse into the spiritual realm, Caroline Sutherland believes she saw an angel.

Angel in the Snow

Most people who claim to have seen an angel report seeing a human form. Usually the figure thought to be an angel appears suddenly, at a time when help is desperately needed, often in answer to prayer. This happened to Barbara Strong early one cold morning in Syracuse, New York.

Although fresh snow covered the icy roads, Barbara Strong had to get to work. A nurse who knew many others would not make it to work because of the weather, she worried that the patients would be in jeopardy. Barbara backed out of her parking space easily, but when she put the car in gear, her tires began to spin. Thinking she could back up and find traction, she put the car in reverse only to spin her tires again. The rocking maneuver soon buried her wheels in icy ruts. She looked across the lighted parking lot hoping to find help, but it was too early for anyone else to be up and about. Barbara closed her eyes and began to pray.

Suddenly there was a tap on her window. "Need any help?" asked a huge, bearded man with a deep voice.

In that early-morning hour, stuck in icy ruts with a strange man tapping at her window, Barbara was frightened. She told the man he was welcome to try, but she stayed inside her locked car. The man walked to the back of the car, lifted the rear wheels

"If someone were to ask me if I had ever seen an angel, I am afraid I could not give a very satisfying answer. But should I be asked if I ever met a messenger of God, then the answer would be an emphatic and unequivocal 'Yes, I have!'"

Claus Westermann

"Just as there's no correct way to experience angels, there's no right way to see them either. They manifest in a myriad of ways to different people."

Alma Daniel, Timothy Wyllie, and Andrew Ramer, *Ask Your Angels* from the ruts and rolled the car forward several yards on its front wheels. When Barbara turned to thank the man, he was gone. She could see no footprints in the brightly lighted parking lot, although a fresh layer of snow covered the ice.

"How could so large a man have crossed the lot twice without leaving a trace? I believe he was an answer to prayer—he was an angel," she says, asking and answering her own question.

Angels Unaware

While some know without a doubt that they have experienced a close encounter with an angel, others don't know exactly what happened. The Bible, in the same verse, both warns and promises that some people will entertain angels without knowing it.

In 1972, Ann Grant's doctor prescribed a month of bed rest in an attempt to avoid surgery for a ruptured disk in her back. However, Ann had two children to get off to school each morning and a husband who traveled frequently. All family members who might help lived more than fourteen hundred miles away. In desperation she answered a cleaning lady's ad in the paper. The cleaning lady agreed to work for Ann one day a week.

"Although we needed help," Ann said, "I worried about having a stranger in the house while I lay in bed."

However, her fear melted away at the sight of Clemy, a smiling lady dressed in a white uniform. "She was beautiful," Ann said, "with a cocoa and peaches complexion, Clemy's black eyes sparkled as she spread joy throughout the house. She actually seemed to make the atmosphere sparkle."

Clemy arrived faithfully every Thursday, week after week. The bed rest proved ineffective, and Ann was forced to undergo surgery and months of recovery. Clemy made the house shine, did all the laundry for a family of four, ironed, and found time in her eight-hour day to arrange flowers for the Grants' dining table.

Then one day, when Ann was about ready to resume her regular duties, Clemy did not arrive for work. Her phone had been disconnected and there was no new number. Clemy seemed to have vanished when the Grants no longer needed her. "I have often wondered about Clemy," Ann said later. "Where did she go? Why didn't she say goodbye? And . . ." she went on, "did we entertain an angel unaware?"

Animal Angels?

Although not as common as encounters with angels in human form, some people believe they have had encounters with animals that are actually angels. John Bosco, an Italian priest who died in 1888 and was canonized (recognized as a saint) in 1934, related such an experience. On his way to an important meeting one evening, a large, gray dog blocked the doorway. As Father Bosco attempted to pass, the dog growled fiercely. After several attempts to leave, the priest gave up and went to bed. The next morning the dog was gone.

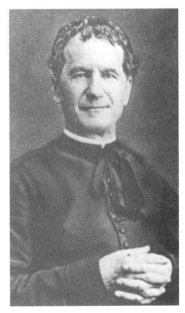

Father John Bosco believed an angel in the form of a fierce gray dog saved his life. This guardian angel prevented Bosco from leaving his house, thereby quelling an assassination attempt.

Later that day Father Bosco received word that he had been the object of an assassination attempt. Throughout the night would-be attackers waited in ambush. Had he left the house he surely would have been killed. The priest believed his guardian angel had taken on the form of the gray dog.

Are All the Stories of Angel Sightings True?

Did all these people actually see angels? Can ordinary-looking people who vanish, bright lights, mysterious dogs, and flowing rainbows all represent the appearance of angels?

K. Martin-Kuri, an artist who is now dedicating her life to the study of angels, says that "angels appear as beings of great light." She believes that angels are nothing but light. However, they reveal themselves to people in a form the person can perceive—a businessperson with a briefcase, a truck driver, a waitress, or even a large, protective dog. "It doesn't matter what their appearance is—you can always feel an essence of peace . . . inner quietness and a sense that they are giving you a blessing."

Ron Rhodes disagrees:

The Bible gives no indication whatsoever that angels appear to humans according to whatever form they are willing to accept. Rather, the visitation of angels typically involves a glorious and awesome appearance that brings fear and trembling to a person.

Dr. Rhodes gives the example of several biblical characters who encountered angels. Daniel was left without strength after seeing an angel. Fear gripped

An angel announces the birth of Jesus to frightened shepherds. While some angelologists believe that angels instill a person with a sense of tranquility, others believe that angels cause a person to tremble with fear.

Zechariah when he saw an angel in the temple, and the shepherds were afraid when the angel appeared to announce the birth of Jesus. Angels appearing in their natural state in the Bible caused fear. Abraham, however, seemed unafraid as he entertained the three angels appearing as men in the shade of an oak tree.

Rabbi Yosef Levin, who lives in Palo Alto, California, contends that actual angel sightings are rare. In his opinion, only people who have lived completely spiritual lives would ever see an angel. And those who actually see an angel would never tell about it. Levin says:

> A person who sees an angel is divinely inspired, . . . entirely holy and humble. And humility is not compatible with going and telling the world you saw an angel. Unless you're a prophet.

Ahmad Sakr, an Islamic scholar living in Los Angeles, agrees that angels allow themselves to be seen only by spiritual people (prophets). However, New Age followers who devoutly believe in angels say sightings and visitations are common in the 1990s because angels recognize how badly humanity needs help in troubled times. In fact, these people not only believe that everyone has a personal guardian angel but also that some people have many angels watching over them. People like Sophy Burnham, author of *A Book of Angels*, believe that angels take pleasure in contact with ordinary humans. Burnham contends that if you want to see an angel, "Just ask for insight and clarity, ask to see and then ask for understanding when you do see."

With so many different views, how can anyone know who is right?

"The evidence for angels seems as ethereal and elusive as the winged creatures themselves."

Joe Nickell, *Entities*

"I believe in angels because the Bible says there are angels; and I believe the Bible to be the true Word of God. I also believe in angels because I have sensed their presence in my life on special occasions."

Billy Graham, *Angels: God's Secret Agents*

Five

What Do Angels Do?

Jews, Christians, and Muslims believe that angels bring messages from God. All three religions credit angels with other activities as well, and each religion sees these activities differently. Within the Christian religion, Catholics and Protestants disagree on the role of angels. Catholics place strong emphasis on guardian angels (angels that protect and watch over individual people), while Protestants lean more toward angel messengers that serve God by helping and protecting his people.

The Protestant view has little focus on angels in daily life, whereas Catholic children are taught to pray daily to their guardian angel. Muslims also believe that angels are active in their daily lives. They believe that each person is accompanied by angels that record his or her deeds. Some Jews believe that every human is accompanied by two angels: that one encourages good and another encourages evil. As a result, each person constantly experiences a good-against-evil struggle within him- or herself.

Angel enthusiasts of the New Age movement agree with many of these religious beliefs. They agree that angels travel back and forth between heaven and earth and have the ability to step instantly from the invisible to the visible world; they

(Opposite page) The function of angels varies in different religions. Catholics believe in guardian angels (pictured) who watch over individual people, while Jews believe that angels cause people to experience a struggle between good and evil.

also agree that angels help and protect people. However, whereas the Abrahamic religions view angels as distinct and separate from both God and humans, the New Age movement believes angels and/or other spiritual guides lead people to a new understanding of becoming one with the universe and one with God.

Author Andrew Ramer conducts workshops to help people learn to communicate with angels. He says an angel has told him that humanity is nearing the next stage of evolution, where the "conscious connection between humans and angels will be the norm." In other words, at some time in the future, everyone will have an awareness of angels and be able to communicate with them.

While followers of the New Age seek new truths in messages from angels, the Abrahamic religions believe that the role of angels is to help people understand the unchanging truths established by God in the beginning.

Angels Praise and Serve God

Christians, Muslims, and Jews believe that angels do most of their work in heaven, where they worship God. The Bible makes many references to angels praising God.

Based on the Scriptures and other sources, Dionysius the Pseudo-Areopagite mapped out the duties for each order of angels. He said that seraphim, the highest order of angels, stand closest to God. The Bible states that they worship and praise God as they constantly circle the throne, chanting, "Holy, Holy, Holy is the Lord Almighty, the whole earth is full of His Glory." The seraphim are considered to be the angels of love, of light, and of fire. Their name in Hebrew means "flaming."

Cherubim, the second-ranking order of angels, radiate the light and knowledge of God. That is, having been given knowledge of the mysteries of God and the depths of his wisdom, they pass this

The Bible asserts that angels constantly circle God's throne, offering praise and worship.

knowledge on to others. *Cherubim*, translated from Hebrew, means "great understanding." According to the Bible, cherubim used flaming swords as they guarded the Tree of Life and the gates to the Garden of Eden after Adam and Eve were evicted.

Thrones, the third order of angels, bring about God's justice. Dionysius called them God-bearing because they bear the grace of God within themselves. Through the thrones, the power of justice comes to earth to help kings and rulers make the right judgments.

"God uses angels to work out the destinies of men and nations."

Billy Graham, *Angels: God's Secret Agents*

"They are our fellow-servants, and our fellow-workers, and they carefully watch over and defend even the humblest of us."

John Cardinal Newman, a leader of the Catholic Church

Dominions, first in the middle triad of angels, rule, or dominate, angels in the lower orders. They reveal the majesty of God and regulate angel duties. In addition, they teach people how to control the human senses (desires and passions) in order to overcome temptation.

Virtues, the second in the middle triad of angels, are filled with divine strength. Members of this order work miracles on earth and act as the chief givers of grace and valor. Through them, worthy saints can receive the ability to work miracles of healing.

Ranking third in the middle triad, powers have power over Satan. They keep the world from being overthrown by evil, and they help individuals in their struggles against evil thoughts.

First in the lower triad, principalities have control over the lowest orders of angels. These angels raise worthy individuals to political office. In this way they protect religion as they watch over leaders and help them reach the right decisions.

Second in the lower triad, archangels bring messages of divine decrees to earth. They are called heralds of good news, and they announce great and glorious events. They receive understanding of God's will from the higher orders of angels and relate it to the lower order, the angels that interact with humans.

Angels, the last order and those closest to people, act as mediators between God and people. They teach people to live virtuously and righteously before God. Guardian angels belong in this rank and are always ready to help people who want their help.

Angel Messengers

The Old and New Testaments, the Koran, and other ancient religious writings contain accounts of messenger angels. Do angels still bring messages to people today? Many people say they do and claim to have received a message from an angel. Sometimes the message comes into their mind. They know the words are a thought transmitted by an angel with a message from God. At other times, a voice is heard so clearly that the person turns to see who is speaking, only to find no one there.

For example, one day Opal Housley, a young farm girl in Oklahoma, decided to add straw to the chicken nests. As she reached to take some straw from the cattle feed trough, she heard someone say, "Stop! There is a snake in the manger."

Guardian angels belong to the last order of angels and mediate between God and humans. In addition to providing protection and guidance, angels in this category teach people to live by God's laws.

Opal looked around. She was the only person in the barn and she saw nothing but straw in the manger. As she reached for straw again, she heard the voice a second time. As before, no one was there and she saw nothing in the straw.

She reached for the straw a third time. Again the voice warned her. This time, certain there was no snake, Opal argued out loud that no snake was there. At that moment the straw began to rustle, and a few seconds later a poisonous snake slithered out.

Opal believes she heard the voice of an angel with a message that saved her life. In this encounter the angel not only brought a message but acted as a guardian as well.

Guardian Angels

Many people, especially Catholics, believe everyone has a guardian angel nearby at all times. A *Time* magazine poll reported 46 percent of people they asked believed they have a guardian angel.

Muslims also believe in the existence of angels who can help and protect them. However, the emphasis in Islam is on self-help rather than on reliance on guardian angels. Muslims believe angels come to the aid of people who strive to do their best on earth. Proof of this striving includes worshiping God, promoting his word, and making a better life for themselves and society.

Some people believe everyone is assigned a specific angel. Others believe hosts of guardian angels exist to serve where they are needed. At any given time one person may be surrounded by many, one, or no angels, depending on the need.

Some of those who do not practice a specific religion find it easy to believe in guardian angels and bypass God and religious experience. A commitment to God requires obedience, but a guardian angel can protect, comfort, and guide without any demands. As a result, guardian angels are extremely popular.

"The faithful service of angels to mankind is not based on their love for you and me. It's based on their love for God."

Landrum Leavell in *A Rustle of Angels*

"But if these beings guard you, they do so because they have been summoned by your prayers."

St. Ambrose, fourth-century Christian leader

Even some nonreligious people find it easy to believe in guardian angels who offer direction and security but do not demand obedience.

If so many people have guardian angels, then why do accidents happen? One explanation is that God created the world along with a set of natural laws that cannot be broken without penalty. For instance, when the natural laws of motion—gravity, speed, and direction—are broken, accidents happen. Considering the number of accidents that occur, it appears that God seldom chooses to overturn his own laws.

Another explanation is that angels strive to protect the spiritual well-being of people more than their physical health. According to this belief, angels may always be acting in a person's best interest even when someone suffers bodily injury in an accident. Perhaps the victim will benefit spiritually in ways they do not understand at the time.

Mere Coincidence or Angelic Intervention?

When accidents almost happen but don't, some people believe it is mere coincidence. Those who believe in guardian angels, however, often credit an angel for their deliverance from danger. Still others wonder, "Was it an angel that saved me?" but they are reluctant to affirm the possibility without proof. Consider the day a car and a large truck loaded with blocks of granite destined to be tombstones approached a narrow country bridge from opposite ends at about the same time. Because of trees and a slight curve in the road, neither driver saw the other until they were past the point of no return and on a collision course. Each driver made an instant decision. Neither applied the brakes. Both steered straight ahead. Miraculously, the vehicles sped past each other safely on the one-lane bridge. Viewing the bridge later, it appeared that even if the outside wheels of each vehicle rode the edge of the wooden bridge there was not room to pass. And yet they did!

Were these people precision stunt car drivers? No, they were residents of a small Oklahoma town. Were they accustomed to maneuvering in heavy traffic? No, in that area of the country they often drove for miles without meeting another car. Who were they? Ordinary people, devout Protestants. They give God credit for their protection, but they do not know whether he sent a guardian angel to protect them or not.

Some who hear the story will be certain the hands of guardian angels guided the vehicles. Others will be just as certain that these drivers controlled their own destiny and used their own driving skills to steer across the narrow bridge. There is no scientific evidence that either of these opinions is right—or wrong.

Angels Enlighten

Some people, mostly followers of the New Age movement, believe that angels reveal information that will change their lives and prepare them for the future. Angels teach them to become more aware of the spiritual realm and help them reach a new level of consciousness, and a better understanding of love, peace, and joy. Stories of angel encounters abound among the followers of the New Age as they strive to open themselves to the angels.

Recurring Patterns

Angel stories seem to have recurring patterns. Many stories involve miraculous escapes from traffic accidents, a lost person being guided to his or her destination, or an angel who suddenly appears to help a stranded motorist. Some people have been protected by armies of angels, while others have crossed through dangerous territory escorted by one or two large bodyguards seen only by their would-be attackers. Still others have been comforted by compassionate angels during times of distress or sorrow.

Skeptics explain the similarity of angel stories as a preconceived way of explaining unusual experiences. In other words, after hearing stories where angels are thought to have been at work, a person may be likely to see angels at work in his or her own experiences. This may fill a need to make sense of unusual events, and at times angels may be the most acceptable answer.

In many stories of angel encounters, sympathetic angels offer comfort and compassion to people in distress or provide protection and rescue from dire straits.

Six

Are Angels Always Good?

"I believe in angels, and I believe that some of these, by the abuse of their free will, have become enemies to God and . . . to us." In 1961 C. S. Lewis, a well-known Christian writer, wrote the preceding comment in the preface to his book *The Screwtape Letters.*

From today's most popular books and current magazine articles on angels, however, one would think the angels wait eagerly for an opportunity to do a kind deed. This image supports the view held by many people that one need only ask, and an angel, closely resembling a fairy godmother, will materialize. Stories of beautiful, kind, gentle, and comforting angels abound today, but the Old Testament presents quite a different image.

185,000 Slain

One Old Testament account from the second Book of Kings, tells how an angel carried out God's judgment. The Assyrian king Sennacherib decided to attack Jerusalem. He made the mistake of sending a letter ahead denouncing the God of Israel. When the message reached King Hezekiah of Israel, he took the letter to the temple and prayed for protection. According to the Bible, that night God sent an angel into the Assyrian camp and the next morning

(Opposite page) Many narratives from the Old Testament recount how angels crushed armies and tempted people to disobey God. This engraving shows Satan and the rebel angels being cast out of heaven by God's army.

70

According to an account from the second Book of Kings, a sword-wielding angel destroyed the army of Sennacherib, an Assyrian king who had denounced the God of Israel.

King Sennacherib awoke to find all his soldiers slain. One angel killed 185,000 soldiers. With no army, Sennacherib fled.

Ancient Hebrew writers believe Michael was the angel who killed the soldiers that night. The image of this mighty and fierce warrior—and most of the angels described in the Old Testament—does not fit the modern angel image of gentle kindness.

Angel experts, including theology scholars and popular authors, disagree on whether all angels act for the good of humankind. Some believe that all angels do the will of God all the time, even when their actions seem contrary to the human view of good. Others believe that some angels are good and some angels are evil. They believe evil, or fallen, angels are cohorts of Satan and are responsible for all the evil in the world.

Temptation of Eve

In support of the view that fallen angels are responsible for evil, the Old Testament describes how evil came into the world. A serpent convinces Eve that she is free to disobey God. Eve yields to temptation and then shares the forbidden fruit with Adam. The third chapter of the Book of Genesis describes God's anger at Adam and Eve's disobedience and how God evicts them from the Garden of Eden. Some religious scholars believe the serpent represents Satan, the fallen angel. If the serpent was Satan in disguise, then angels are not always good.

The Adversary

In the Old Testament, Satan, the fallen angel, is humanity's adversary, not God's. (The name *Satan* means "adversary" in Hebrew.) He acts according to God's will when he tempts humans. The Book of Job (rhymes with robe) tells how Satan appears before God with the other angels. God asks where he has been, and Satan replies that he has been roaming about the earth. God asks if he has noticed his servant Job. Satan says he has, but that Job would not be such a good servant if God didn't make life so easy for him.

In order to prove Job's faithfulness, God allows Satan to bring extreme hardship upon Job. Satan causes one disaster after another. Raiders steal Job's livestock and kill his servants. His children die in a windstorm. Finally, Job breaks out with painful

This fifteenth-century woodcut depicts both the temptation of Eve and the eviction of Adam and Eve from the Garden of Eden.

sores from head to toe. Through all this suffering Job remains faithful to God. In this example, Satan plays the role of adversary. He makes bad things happen to good people, but he has God's approval.

Fallen Angels

Although the Bible says more about what Satan does than where he came from, Christians believe he is a fallen angel. Christian theologians as well as secular writers have many opinions on when and how the fall occurred. The poet Dante reasons that the fall took place less than twenty seconds after God created the angels. Milton, in *Paradise Lost*, placed the angelic creation and fall just before the temptation of Eve in the Garden of Eden. The most widely accepted Christian view places the time of the fall before the creation of the world, soon after God created the angels.

Some Christians see a connection between verses in the Old Testament's Book of Ezekiel and the New Testament's Book of Revelation. They believe the following verses describe the fall of Satan.

Many Christians believe that Satan, the adversary of humanity and the leader of the dark angels, reigns over the souls of sinners.

Ezekiel 28:

12. Son of man, take up a lament concerning the king of Tyre and say to him: This is what the Sovereign Lord says: You were the model of perfection, full of wisdom and perfect in beauty.

13. You were in Eden, the garden of God; every precious stone adorned you: ruby, topaz and emerald, chrysolite, onyx and jasper, sapphire, turquoise and beryl. Your settings and mountings were made of gold; on the day you were created they were prepared.

14. You were anointed as a guardian cherub, for so I ordained you. You were on the holy mount of God; you walked among the fiery stones.

15. You were blameless in your ways from the day you were created till wickedness was found in you.

16. Through your widespread trade you were filled with violence, and you sinned. So I drove you in disgrace from the mount of God, and I expelled you, O guardian cherub, from among the fiery stones.

17. Your heart became proud on account of your beauty, and you corrupted your wisdom because of your splendor. So I threw you to the earth; I made a spectacle of you before kings.

Revelation 12:

7. And there was war in heaven. Michael and his angels fought against the dragon; and the dragon and his angels fought back.

8. But he was not strong enough, and they lost their place in heaven.

9. The great dragon was hurled down—that ancient serpent called the devil, or Satan, who leads the whole world astray. He was hurled to the earth, and his angels with him.

According to these verses, Michael and the holy angels fought against Lucifer (now known as Satan) and the angels that followed him. Satan lost the battle and was cast out of heaven along with his angels. Because they fell from heaven, these angels, including Satan, are known as fallen angels. Other verses indicate that about one-third of the angels God created fell. Some were held prisoner in hell while others fell to earth. These are dark angels or fallen angels.

Billy Graham believes Lucifer's revolt against God and the fall of the rebellious angels was the greatest catastrophe of all time. Many Christians believe the fall of the angels was the birth of evil.

Graham and other theologians believe that verses in the New Testament describing Satan and the fallen angels as enemies of God clarify the meaning of Old Testament verses concerning Satan. Others, including modern Bible scholar Charles Ryrie, argue that the verses in Ezekiel do not refer

"We believe that angels are messengers of God, and that they have no evil inclination."

Rabbi Yosef Levin in "Look Earthward, Angel"

"The greatest catastrophe in the history of the universal creation was Lucifer's defiance of God and the consequent fall of perhaps one-third of the angels who joined him in his wickedness."

Billy Graham, *Angels: God's Secret Agents*

In the New Testament's Book of Revelation, Michael and his army of angels fought against Satan and his rebels. The victorious Michael is believed to have sent Satan hurling to the earth in defeat.

to Satan, but to the king of Tyre, a *man* under the influence of Satan.

Judaism

Some Jews believe that all angels, including Satan, are good angels that do the work of God. However, angels sometimes test people by tempting them to do wrong. A person who is tempted by an angel must choose between right and wrong. According to Jewish beliefs, these tests bring out the best in people.

Rabbi Yosef Levin of Chabad in Palo Alto, the local branch of the international Chabad Lubavitch

Hassidic movement, says, "There are angels that carry out the good and angels that carry out the evil, to give us free choice. Even Satan is doing God's will. God is testing us to bring out our best."

According to Rabbi Levin, the human soul that serves God can soar to greater spiritual heights than an angel. The good deeds one does on earth affect the worlds above, bringing holiness and light.

Popular Views of Dark Angels

In the press, guardian angels generally receive more attention today than fallen angels do. Eileen Freeman, publisher of *AngelWatch* newsletter, admits that stories of evil angels are plentiful, but she refuses to give them space in her newsletter. She keeps the focus of her newsletter on the good works angels do. C. S. Lewis, however, wrote about bad angels and their influence on people. He said, "They do not differ in nature from good angels, but their nature is depraved. Devil is the opposite of angel only as Bad Man is the opposite of Good Man."

Readers of adult fiction have long been fascinated with horror stories dealing with fallen angels and other supernaturally evil creatures. As a result, the works of Stephen King, John Saul, and Anne Rice, which often deal with these subjects, are often on best-seller lists. More recently, the juvenile horror works of Christopher Pike and R. L. Stine have taken over the juvenile best-seller lists.

Some people wonder why these books and movies are so popular. For one thing, these books take the reader on a literary roller coaster ride, and almost everyone likes a thrill. In addition, when the threat is imaginary, fear is fun. Some psychologists say that the scary but unbelievable characters in horror books and movies may actually soothe fears of the unknown by making it easy to deny the possibility that real demons exist.

The evil creatures that lurk on the pages of horror books and creep from the shadows in horror

In this 1496 woodcut, the Lord and Satan vie for a man's soul. Jews believe that angels sometimes test people's faith in God by tempting them to choose between good and evil.

films are usually ugly and terrifying. The biblical Satan, however, is a creature of beauty. This attractive master deceiver is likely to appear with a message that everything will be wonderful if we only do as he says. Unfortunately, he leaves a trail of destroyed lives and demolished futures. According to Billy Graham, "Satan and his demons are known by the discord they promote, the wars they start, the hatred they engender, the murders they initiate. . . . They are dedicated to the spirit of destruction." In the New Testament, the apostle Paul warns that fallen angels masquerade as angels of light. In other words, these evil angels do not appear to be evil.

Some say fallen angels contribute to the world's evil. If so, the evening news dramatically records their deeds; crime, hatred, disease, and war fill the pages of our newspapers and the hours of television news. But do those who commit vicious deeds act out of free will or under spiritual influence?

In the Christian view, Satan is a deceiver with an army of fallen angels at his command. He plays mind games. With persuasive tactics, he can make almost anything seem acceptable. He twists the truth, sometimes to the point that wrong seems right. According to the Bible, God gave humans the right to choose. Consequently, although evil forces may influence human behavior, people cannot blame spiritual forces for their own misdeeds. The right choice is always available even though temptation may lead in the other direction.

Continual Rivalry

Some believe evil spirits continually war with God and his people. Others believe God remains in control of spirit beings that carry out seemingly evil deeds, and also that crime, sickness, accidents, and so forth work toward an outcome that is ultimately good. We have few clues to help solve this mystery.

One source of information is a document found among the recently discovered Dead Sea scrolls, en-

"The angels . . . regard our safety, undertake our defense, direct our ways . . . [so] that no evil befalls us."

John Calvin, sixteenth-century French theologian

"The evil angels are also at work trying to influence each person. . . . We humans are caught in the crossfire."

Marilynn Carlson Webber and William D. Webber, *A Rustle of Angels*

Some believe that Satan and the fallen angels (pictured) perpetually wage war against God and humanity.

titled "The War of the Sons of Light Against the Sons of Darkness." In this ancient writing, the angel Michael is called the Prince of Light. He leads the angels of light into battle against the angels of darkness, who are led by the demon Balial.

Evangelist Billy Graham, and many others, believe an ongoing battle exists between good and evil. "We live in a perpetual battlefield—the great War of the Ages continues to rage," says Graham. This age-old battle continues, as holy angels and the fallen angels battle for control, not only for the will of each person, but for the governments of the world. According to this belief, unseen forces are at work trying to destroy the church, topple Christian governments, and doom human souls to hell. This war will be concluded only at the end of the world when Jesus Christ returns. At that time the final battle will be fought and Satan will be defeated.

Seven

Do Angels Exist?

According to a 1994 Gallup poll, 72 percent of the Americans who responded believe that angels exist. Five percent of those who believe angels exist also believe they have encountered an angel and claim to have seen, heard, or been rescued by an angel. By popular vote, it seems, angels are real.

This popular belief, however, comes from the heart and not the head. With little conclusive scientific evidence about angels, great thinkers have debated their existence at length.

The ancient philosophers Aristotle and Plato believed that angels exist. Aristotle called them intelligences. Plato saw a relation between the human soul and angelic beings. Socrates, another early philosopher, who believed in nothing that could not be proved by logic and experience, followed the guidance of a spirit he called Daimon. Acting in the manner of a guardian angel, the voice of Daimon warned Socrates whenever he was about to make a bad decision.

Arguments Against the Existence of Angels

In the debate over the existence of angels, scientists and philosophers have followed the guidelines of William of Ockham, one of the most important philosopher-theologians of the Middle Ages. According to Ockham's guideline, the existence of

something that cannot be perceived can only be confirmed if it explains an occurrence that cannot be explained any other way.

For example, magnetic force cannot be seen, touched, heard, smelled, or tasted. Human senses cannot perceive it. Yet the human senses can witness its effects; the eye can see a magnet pulling iron filings from sand. A person can feel the tug of this invisible force by holding a magnet in one hand and an iron object in the other. The senses can detect only the effects, not the actual force. According to Ockham's guidelines, the existence of magnetic force can be confirmed because there is no other way to explain why a magnet attracts iron.

However, scientists have found nothing that cannot be explained unless angels exist. In other words, according to the scientific mind, there is nothing known to have happened (outside the Scriptures) that can be explained only as the work of angels.

Explaining Extraordinary Occurrences

Where angel activity has been suspected, some other possible explanation has surfaced to satisfy the scientific mind. Sometimes the extraordinary occurrence is explained simply as coincidence. Other times a more complex possibility is offered. Take, for example, a person who is brought back from the grip of death who claims to have seen angels during what is commonly called a near-death experience. The person's heartbeat stops for a time and starts again, usually due to outstanding emergency medical care. Some people who have had near-death experiences remember leaving their bodies and traveling through a tunnel toward a bright light and into the presence of angels. The people return to their bodies when the heartbeat resumes. Is this an occurence that cannot be explained unless angels exist?

According to Dr. Sherwin B. Nuland, author of *How We Die*, it is not. He cites the possibility that chemicals produced in the brain cause hallucina-

"An angel is a spiritual creature without a body created by God for the service of Christendom and the church."

Martin Luther, sixteenth-century German theologian

"They [angels] are not . . . anything more than false and insubstantial creation of the restless human imagination."

Robert A. Baker in *Entities*

tions during near-death experiences. During acute stress, especially when the body experiences a major blood loss, the brain produces morphinelike compounds called endorphins. The sudden presence of large amounts of endorphins in the brain has about the same effect as a similar amount of a narcotic such as morphine.

According to Dr. Nuland, "It produces . . . for many people, a certain serenity, and for other people, even certain kinds of hallucinatory phenomena." In other words, people who see angels while under great stress may actually be under the influence of a strong narcotic manufactured by their own brain. As a result, they see visions produced within their own minds. In Nuland's view, the near-death experience takes place within the mind. The spirit does not leave the body and is not escorted into the spirit world by angels.

Professor emeritus Robert A. Baker agrees that angels, along with numerous other supernatural entities, are products of the "ever-active, image-creating human mind." The mind creates these beings to meet a human need or cope with crisis. A lonely child may invent a playmate; a lonely adult may conjure up a beautiful angel to lavish him or her with love.

Professor Baker suggests that belief in life after death is also a creation of the human mind. He says, "When we discover death . . . our minds rebel and invent a soul and an afterlife with a heaven." Fearful people may create guardian angels to protect themselves in today's crime-ridden culture. Moreover, sightings of these mind-creations may result from taking psychedelic drugs, or they may occur naturally during stress. Is it a mere coincidence that angel sightings often occur at times of great fear, severe injury, serious illness, or dire hardship?

Arguments for the Existence of Angels

St. Thomas Aquinas, thirteenth-century Roman Catholic theologian, declared that "the universe

Some scientists believe that the human mind invents images of angels to help people cope during times of loneliness and hardship.

would be incomplete without [angels]." He further explained that God created angels to make a perfect universe. According to his thinking, a perfect universe "must not lack any nature that can possibly exist." He also reasoned that a perfect universe also requires an orderly arrangement of things. This orderly arrangement involves a progressive chain of being. Aquinas placed lifeless and mindless objects like rocks and dust at the bottom of the chain. These were followed by plants, life without minds. Next he placed animals and humans, living creatures with minds. These were followed by minds without bodies—angels, the necessary link between humans and God in an orderly universe. To prove this view, Aquinas insisted that without angels there would be an obvious gap between humans and God.

The poet Dante, in his *Convivio*, extended Aquinas's reasoning. He declared that in an orderly universe, the progression "is by almost continuous steps, from the lowest form to the highest and from the highest to the lowest." In other words, in the order of things, the difference between the human species and the highest species of animals is about the same as the difference between angels and humans. If we were somehow able to measure the differences between each level in the chain of being (angel, human, beast, bird, fish, insect, microbe, dust), we would find steps of equal distance. If any one of them were missing, a gap would be apparent. In all the visible world we see no gaps.

John Locke, a seventeenth-century English philosopher, explained the chain of being this way:

> Down from us the descent is by easy steps. . . . There are some brutes [animals] that seem to have as much reason and knowledge as some that are called men; and the animal and vegetable kingdoms are so nearly joined that, if you will take the lowest of one and the highest of the other, there will scarce be perceived any great difference between them.

Locke concluded that considering all things known about the nature of God, there is reason to think that "the species of creatures should also, by gentle degrees, ascend upwards from us . . . as we see them gradually descend from us downwards."

This theory supports the *probability* that angels exist but does not prove their *actual* existence.

UFOs

Some people seek an alternative answer. Evolutionary thinkers promote the idea that there are forms of life more highly developed than humans.

"I don't believe that the existence of angels can be proven, but I think there is a significant amount of circumstantial evidence that would persuade an open-minded person."

John Ronner, Tennessee writer

"Because the world we live in is such a fearful, dangerous, and unpredictable place, quite frequently we are driven to invent protectors for ourselves. . . . Haunted by our fears, we create a host of guardian angels to protect us from worldly harm."

Robert A. Baker in *Entities*

Possibly the beings we call angels are in reality more highly developed inhabitants of another planet or even another universe. Those who lean toward this idea see a link between angel sightings and unidentified flying objects, or UFOs.

Reports of angel appearances and visitors from outer space (called extraterrestrials or ETs) contain many similarities. For example, both angels and ETs travel mysteriously through the air and arrive from other worlds—unseen, distant, and mysterious. Angels and ETs are thought to be superior beings. Angels and ETs usually communicate in the language of those who see them and often deliver messages.

Nevertheless, vast differences exist between angels and ETs. ETs travel by spaceship, but angels seem to appear and disappear with no visible means of transportation. ETs and their spaceships seem to have physical bodies unlike anything on earth, while angels are often perceived as spirits that assume bodies common to earth.

Ezekiel's Vision

Some people suggest that an account in the Old Testament's Book of Ezekiel describes a UFO sighting related to an angel appearance.

Ezekiel 1:

4. I looked, and I saw a windstorm coming out of the north—an immense cloud with flashing lightning and surrounded by brilliant light. The center of the fire looked like glowing metal,

5. and in the fire was what looked like four living creatures. In appearance their form was that of a man,

6. but each of them had four faces and four wings.

7. Their legs were straight; their feet were like those of a calf and gleamed like burnished bronze.

Many similarities exist between reports of angel appearances and extraterrestrial sightings. An account in the Old Testament describes one such incident in which strange beings, wheels, and whirling lights appeared to Ezekiel.

8. Under their wings on their four sides they had the hands of a man. All four of them had faces and wings,

9. and their wings touched one another. Each one went straight ahead; they did not turn as they moved.

10. Their faces looked like this: Each of the four had the face of a man, and on the right side each had the face of a lion, and on the left the face of an ox; each also had the face of an eagle.

11. Such were their faces. Their wings were spread out upward; each had two wings, one touching the wing of another creature on either side, and two wings covering its body.

12. Each one went straight ahead. Wherever the spirit would go, they would go, without turning as they went.

13. The appearance of the living creatures was like burning coals of fire or like torches. Fire moved back and forth among the creatures; it was bright, and lightning flashed out of it.

14. The creatures sped back and forth like flashes of lightning.

86

15. As I looked at the living creatures, I saw a wheel on the ground beside each creature with its four faces.

16. This was the appearance and structure of the wheels. They sparkled like chrysolite, and all four looked alike. Each appeared to be made like a wheel intersecting a wheel.

17. As they moved, they would go in any one of the four directions the creatures faced; the wheels did not turn about as the creatures went.

18. Their rims were high and awesome, and all four rims were full of eyes all around.

19. When the living creatures moved, the wheels beside them moved; and when the living creatures rose from the ground, the wheels also rose.

20. Wherever the spirit would go, they would go, and the wheels would rise along with them, because the spirit of the living creatures was in the wheels.

21. When the creatures moved, they also moved; when the creatures stood still, they also stood still; and when the creatures rose from the ground, the wheels rose along with them, because the spirit of the living creatures was in the wheels.

22. Spread out above the heads of the living creatures was what looked like an expanse, sparkling like ice, and awesome.

23. Under the expanse their wings were stretched out one toward the other, and each had two wings covering its body.

24. When the creatures moved, I heard the sound of their wings, like the roar of rushing waters, like the voice of the Almighty, like the tumult of an army. When they stood still, they lowered their wings.

25. Then there came a voice from above the expanse over their heads as they stood with lowered wings.

"For some, their faith doesn't have room for such creatures. . . . They can't believe things that aren't literal, that are outside the five senses."

Reverend John Westerhoff, pastoral theologian at Duke University's Divinity School

"The existence of angels is one of the pillars of belief in most religious traditions and that is the case in Islam also."

Shaykh Hisham Kabbani, author of *Angels Unveiled: A Sufi Perspective*

26. Above the expanse over their heads was what looked like a throne of sapphire, and high above on the throne was a figure like that of a man.

27. I saw that from what appeared to be his waist up he looked like glowing metal, as if full of fire, and that from there down he looked like fire; and brilliant light surrounded him.

28. Like the appearance of a rainbow in the clouds on a rainy day, so was the radiance around him. This was the appearance of the likeness of the glory of the LORD. When I saw it, I fell facedown, and I heard the voice of one speaking.

Continued Debate

Some scholars reason that Ezekiel's descriptions of wheels, strange beings, and lights whirling in the air might be the way a man who lived in a time when rotating devices belonged on oxcarts, not helicopters or planes, might describe a spaceship. Others believe Ezekiel recorded an angelic appearance with a description of cherubim.

No one can prove that either angels or extraterrestrials exist. The existence of one, angels, is based on faith, and the existence of the other, ETs, on speculation. Possibly the most significant difference between angels and ETs may be that angels are thought to reside in heaven, where they worship and serve God, and ETs are thought to live on a distant planet, more like our equal in the vast universe than a link between humans and God.

The debate goes on. Although many have tried, no one has proved that angels exist. Furthermore, it may be far more difficult to alter the view of those who believe than to sway the nonbeliever. What evidence can stand against faith that somehow opens the door for contact with these spiritual beings from the celestial realm? Even though their existence cannot be proved, who would not like to believe that a guardian angel hovers nearby?

Afterword

Proving the Impossible

In a time when people are caught up in angelmania, angels are a hot commerical item. Controversy over their existence, however, is not. I recently posted several messages about angels on Internet newsgroups, where flaming (angry response) is an art. My messages resulted in enthusiastic reports of angel experiences and many simple acknowledgements of belief. The occasional mild "angels do not exist" statement did not even receive replies. People seem to accept almost all views of angels. Varying explanations of what or who angels are stir no controversy.

In the 1990s, it has become acceptable to talk freely about angels, the mysterious messengers from God. Popular acceptance of angels has given many people who believe they have encountered angels the courage to speak out. Some say an angel "changed my life," or "saved my child." Others believe that they have met a spiritual guide who is leading them to a higher understanding that will change the world. Still others open businesses where the invisible spirits hang out.

Talk about fallen angels or dark spirits is not as open as talk about gentle angels. Nevertheless, many people have a strong interest in the fictitious accounts of darkness found in horror novels and

(Opposite page) Regardless of a lack of evidence, many people continue to believe in the existence of angels.

movies. Yet, many fear that they may encounter a dark spirit masquerading as an angel of light.

The existence of angels is impossible to prove and equally difficult to dispute. Scholars and great thinkers have tried to do both. The real mystery is not whether angels exist, or even who or what they are, but why so many people, almost since time began, believe in their existence. Few believers care that the existence of angels cannot be proved; they know what they believe.

For Further Exploration

Joan Wester Anderson, *Where Angels Walk*. Sea Cliff, NY: Barton & Brett, 1992.

Denise Brumbach, "Angel in Our Backyard," *Guideposts*, May 1995.

Sophy Burnham, *A Book of Angels*. New York: Ballantine Books, 1990.

Eileen Elias Freeman, *Touched by Angels*. New York: Warner Books, 1993.

Nancy Gibbs and Howard G. Chua-Eoan, "Angels Among Us," *Time*, December 27, 1993.

Cecelia Goodnow, "An Angel on Your Shoulder," *San Francisco Examiner*, August 25, 1993.

C. S. Lewis, *The Screwtape Letters*. New York: Macmillan, 1961.

Morris B. Margolies, *A Gathering of Angels*. New York: Ballantine Books, 1994.

Dawn Raffel, "Angels All Around Us," *Redbook*, December 1992.

Richard Scheinin, "Look Earthward, Angel: Winged Messengers of Bible and Lore," *San Jose Mercury News*, June 5, 1993.

Charlie W. Shedd, *Brush of an Angel's Wing*. Ann Arbor, MI: Servant Publications, 1994.

Works Consulted

Mortimer J. Adler, *The Angels and Us*. New York: Macmillan, 1982.

Trudy Bush, "On the Tide of the Angels," *The Christian Century*, March 1, 1995.

Alma Daniel, Timothy Wyllie, and Andrew Ramer, *Ask Your Angels*. New York: Ballantine Books, 1992.

Erich von Däniken, *In Search of Ancient Gods*. New York: G. P. Putnam's Sons, 1974.

Gastav Davidson, *A Dictionary of Angels*. New York: Free Press, 1967.

Enid Gauldie, "Flights of Angels," *History Today*, December 1992.

Malcolm Godwin, *Angels: An Endangered Species*. New York: Simon and Schuster, 1990.

Billy Graham, *Angels: God's Secret Agents*. Dallas: Word Publishing, 1975, 1986.

Susan Hall-Balduf, "Angel Aware: Graceful Stories from Heavens Afar," *Detroit Free Press*, December 15, 1993.

Rex Hauck, ed., *Angels: The Mysterious Messengers*. New York: Ballantine Books, 1994.

The Holy Bible, King James Version (KJV)

The Holy Bible, New International Version (NIV)

Timothy Jones and Andrew J. Bandstra, "Rumors of Angels?" *Christianity Today*, April 5, 1993.

Barbara Kantrowitz et al., "In Search of the Sacred," *Newsweek*, November 28, 1994.

Gary Kinnaman, *Angels Dark and Light*. Ann Arbor, MI: Servant Publications, 1994.

The Koran Interpreted. Arthur J. Arberry, trans. New York: Collier Books, 1955.

Richard McBrien, "Comfort, Help of Angels May Hover Close at Hand," *National Catholic Reporter*, March 4, 1994.

Mrs. St. John Mildmay, "Phantom Armies Seen in France," *North American Review*, August 1915.

————, "Those Angels at Mons," *Literary Digest*, September 25, 1915.

James Patrick Moroney, "Saints and Angels: Our Companions on Life's Journey," *The Catholic World*, March/April 1995.

Joe Nickell, *Entities*. Buffalo, NY: Prometheus Books, 1995.

James N. Pruitt, *The Complete Angel*. New York: Avon Books, 1995.

Ron Rhodes, *Angels Among Us*. Eugene, OR: Harvest House Publishers, 1994.

Debora Vrana, "Family Copes with Grief by Believing in Angels," *Los Angeles Times*, December 13, 1993.

Theodora Ward, *Men and Angels*. New York: Viking Press, 1969.

Marilynn Carlson Webber and William D. Webber, *A Rustle of Angels*. Grand Rapids, MI: Zondervan Publishing House, 1994.

Craig Wilson, "Hark and Hallelujah! The Angels Are Here," *San Jose Mercury News*, October 28, 1992.

Index

About the Author

Deanne Durrett is the author of three other non-fiction books for Lucent—*Organ Transplants* (1993), *The Importance of Jim Henson* (1994), and *The Importance of Norman Rockwell* (1997), as well as a middle-grade novel, *My New Sister the Bully*, published by Abingdon Press. She has published stories and articles in magazines for adults as well as children and newspaper feature stories, commentary, and columns. She retired as San Diego regional adviser for the Society of Children's Book Writers and Illustrators in 1994 after serving five and a half years.

Picture Credits